PREACHING
FOR
GOD'S
GLORY

TODAY'S
ISSUES

PREACHING

FOR

GOD'S

GLORY

ALISTAIR
BEGG

CROSSWAY BOOKS • WHEATON, ILLINOIS
A DIVISION OF GOOD NEWS PUBLISHERS

Preaching for God's Glory

Published by Crossway Books
  a division of Good News Publishers
  1300 Crescent Street
  Wheaton, Illinois 60187

First printing, 1999

Printed in the United States of America

The Alliance of Confessing Evangelicals exists to call the
church, amidst our dying culture, to repent of its worldli-
ness, to recover and confess the truth of God's Word as
did the Reformers, and to see that truth embodied in doctrine, worship and life.

Library of Congress Cataloging-in-Publication Data
Begg, Alistair.
  Preaching for God's Glory / Alistair Begg.
  p.   cm. — (Today's issues)
  Includes bibliographical references.
  ISBN 1-58134-123-7
  1. Preaching. 2. Bible—Homiletical use. I. Title. II. Series:
Today's Issues (Wheaton, Ill.)
BV4211.2.B43 2000
251—dc21   99-36911
                                                      CIP

15	14	13	12	11	10	09	08	07	06	05	04	03	02	01
15	14	13	12	11	10	9	8	7	6	5	4	3	2	

CONTENTS

PREFACE

These are not good days for the evangelical church, and anyone who steps back from what is going on for a moment to try to evaluate our life and times will understand that.

In the last few years a number of important books have been published all trying to understand what is happening, and they are saying much the same thing even though the authors come from fairly different backgrounds and are doing different work. One is by David F. Wells, a theology professor at Gordon-Conwell Theological Seminary in Massachusetts. It is called *No Place for Truth*. A second is by Michael Scott Horton, vice president of the Alliance of Confessing Evangelicals. His book is called *Power Religion*. The third is by the well-known pastor of Grace Community Church in California, John F. MacArthur. It is called *Ashamed of the Gospel*. Each of these authors is writing about the evangelical church, not the liberal church, and a person can get an idea of what each is saying from the titles alone.

Yet the subtitles are even more revealing. The subtitle of Wells's book reads *Or Whatever Happened to Evangelical Theology?* The subtitle of Horton's book is *The Selling Out of the Evangelical Church*. The subtitle of John MacArthur's work proclaims, *When the Church Becomes Like the World*.

When you put these together, you realize that these careful observers of the current church scene perceive that today evangelicalism is seriously off base because it has abandoned its evangelical truth-heritage. The thesis of David Wells's book is that the evangelical church is either dead or dying as a significant religious force because it has forgotten what it stands for. Instead of trying to do God's work in God's way, it is trying to build a prosperous earthly kingdom with secular tools. Thus, in spite of our apparent success we have been "living in a fool's paradise," Wells declared in an address to the National Association of Evangelicals in 1995.

John H. Armstrong, a founding member of the Alliance of Confessing Evangelicals, has edited a volume titled *The Coming Evangelical Crisis*. When he was asked not long afterwards whether he thought the crisis was still coming or is actually here, he admitted that in his judgment the crisis is already upon us.

The Alliance of Confessing Evangelicals is addressing this problem through seminars and conferences, radio programs, *modern* REFORMATION magazine, Reformation Societies, and scholarly writings. The series of booklets on today's issues is a further effort along these same lines. If you are troubled by the state of today's church and are helped by these booklets, we invite you to contact the Alliance at 1716 Spruce Street, Philadelphia, PA 19103. You can also phone us at 215-546-3696 or visit the Alliance at our website: www.AllianceNet. org. We would like to work with you under God "for a modern Reformation."

James Montgomery Boice
President, Alliance of Confessing Evangelicals
Series Editor, Today's Issues

ONE

The Eclipse of Expository Preaching

I have a vivid recollection as a small boy of sitting in St. George's Tron Church in Glasgow waiting for the commencement of morning worship. At about three minutes to 11 the beadle (parish official) would climb the pulpit stairs and place a large Bible on the lectern. Having opened it to the appropriate passage, he would descend, and the minister would in turn ascend the stairs and sit in the cone-shaped pulpit. The beadle would complete his responsibilities by climbing the stairs a second time to close the pulpit door and leave the pastor to his task. There was no doubt in my young mind that each part of that procedure was marked with significance. There was clearly no reason for the pastor to be in the pulpit apart from the Bible upon which he looked down as he read. I understood that, in contrast to his physical posture, the preacher was standing under Scripture, not over it. Similarly, we were listening not so much for *his* message but for *its* message. We were discovering, as J. I. Packer has suggested, that preaching is "letting texts talk." The right preaching of the Word of God is powerful!

Although D. Martyn Lloyd-Jones voiced his concerns about a certain literary style of Scottish preaching, he would not have disputed the following observation by James W. Alexander: "Among the Scottish Presbyterians every man and every woman, nay, almost every child, carried his pocket-Bible to church, and not only looked out the text, but verified each citation; and as the preaching was in great part of the expository kind, the necessary consequence was, that the whole population became intimately acquainted with the structure of every book in the Bible, and were able to recall every passage with its appropriate accompanying truths" (*Thoughts on Preaching* [Edinburgh and Carlisle, Pa.: Banner of Truth, reprint 1975], p. 240).

Long ago the godly Richard Baxter reminded his fellow pastors of the central place of preaching in the fulfillment of their duties:

> We must be serious, earnest, and zealous in every part of our work. Our work requireth greater skill, and especially greater life and zeal, than any of us bring to it. It is no small matter to stand up in the face of the congregation, and to deliver a message of salvation or damnation, as from the living God, in the name of the Redeemer. It is no easy matter to speak so plain, that the most ignorant may understand us; and so seriously that the deadest heart may feel us; and so convincingly, that the contradicting cavillers may be silenced. (*The Reformed Pastor* [Edinburgh and Carlisle, Pa.: Banner of Truth, reprint 1974], p. 117)

In the Shadows

Unfortunately, Baxter's challenge seems to be beyond the skill and will of most contemporary preachers with the result that true expository preaching has fallen on hard times. About fifty years ago W. E. Sangster, a great Methodist preacher in Britain, began a volume on preaching with the words, "Preaching is in the shadows. The world does not believe in it" (*The Craft of the Sermon* [Harrisburg, Pa.: Epworth Press, 1954], p. 1). Today, at the beginning of a new millennium, the situation is graver still. Preaching is still in the shadows, but this time *much of the church does not believe in it*.

Much of what now emanates from contemporary pulpits would not have been recognized by either Alexander or Baxter or Sangster as being anywhere close to the kind of expository preaching that is Bible-based, Christ-focused, and life-changing—the kind of preaching that is marked by doctrinal clarity, a sense of gravity, and convincing argument. We have instead become far too familiar with preaching that pays scant attention to the Bible, is self-focused, and consequently is capable of only the most superficial impact upon the lives of listeners. Worse still, large sections of the church are oblivious to the fact that they are being administered a placebo rather than the medicine they need. They are satisfied with the feeling that it has done them some good, a feeling that disguises the seriousness of the situation. In the absence of bread the population grows accustomed to cake! Pulpits are for preachers. We build stages for performers.

Some years ago I enjoyed the privilege of speaking at a convention in Hong Kong. The meetings were held in an Anglican church that had a pulpit we did not use. The organizers felt it would be best if we were not six feet above the congregation but on the same level as the people. So they provided a lectern to hold the preacher's Bible as he spoke. I was sharing the event with a kindly older man whom I had never met prior to the convention. We both spoke each morning. Some mornings I would preach first, sometimes he would. Whenever he began a message, his first action was to pick up the small lectern and move it off to the side where it could neither impede his movement nor create the impression that he was "preaching" to the people. Instead, he said, he was delivering a talk, and he wanted to be sure the listeners could relax and benefit from his conversational style. When it came time for me to preach, my first action was to put the lectern back in its place, central to the occasion. The congregation laughed as this pattern repeated itself over the course of five days. I would use it; my colleague would remove it.

Before the week was out, two incidents occurred that may or may not have been related. First, I explained to the congregation that the reason I replaced the lectern each time was not simply so I might have a place for my Bible, but because I did not want to forgo the symbolism of having a central pulpit with the Word in its deserved primary place. After all, I observed, if the preacher were to fall down or disappear, the congregation would still be left with its focus in the right place—namely, the Scriptures. I know that my preaching partner did not take this as a personal rebuke, which is what made the second incident all the more telling.

A day or two later he confided to me that he felt he had lost any real sense of passion or power in the delivery of his messages. It was very humbling for me as a young man to sit and listen as he poured out his heart and with tears reflected upon his diminished zeal. It is far too simplistic to suggest that his removal of the podium each time he spoke was a symbol of a faltering conviction regarding the priority and power of Scripture. But at the same time I have a suspicion that its removal was more than simply a matter of style or personal preference.

The layout of many contemporary church buildings, including my own, at least flirts with the danger of creating the impression that we have come to hear from man rather than to meet with

God. It is imperative that we acknowledge and remember, and help each other acknowledge and remember, that we gather together as the church not to enjoy preaching eloquence (or to criticize its lack) but to hear and heed the Word of God. We come to be exhorted, not entertained.

Caricatures of True Preaching

If churches or their pastors begin to think of the place from which messages are delivered to the congregation as a stage, it is inevitable that caricatures of the preacher will emerge to take the true preacher's place. Sadly, this is precisely what has happened. In our day the expositor of Scripture has been eclipsed by a variety of sad substitutions. We will consider a few.

1. *The cheerleader.* This well-meaning fellow has a peculiar need to be liked and accepted. Whatever the context of a particular message, he is going to be positively inspirational. A good Sunday for him is one where his people laugh a lot, are affirmed and affirming, and go away more self-assured than when they arrived. Whether they were confronted by the truth of God's Word or humbled by God's presence is largely lost sight of in a quest for wholeness that replaces a concern about holiness. Such an individual often leaves the teaching of the Bible to small groups or home studies. The preacher's task, he feels, is to "pump them up" and prepare them for the daunting week that awaits them as soon as they leave the building.

Sadly, in such a case the sheep leave stirred but without being strengthened, and when the sugar fix provided by the milk-shake sermon has worn off, those with any kind of spiritual appetite wander off in search of more substantial food for their souls. The proper work of the preacher is thus not done.

2. *The conjurer.* When we hear the congregation declaring, "Wasn't it amazing what he got out

of that?" we should not immediately assume that the news is good. When the preacher refuses to do the hard work of discovering the actual meaning of the text in its context, and when he divorces discovery and application, just about anything can be conveyed—and often is!

R. W. Dale referred to this in his lectures on preaching given to the faculty and students of Yale in 1876:

> I always think of the tricks of those ingenious gentlemen who entertain the public by rubbing a sovereign between their hands till it becomes a canary, and drawing out of their coat sleeves half a dozen brilliant glass globes filled with water, and with four or five goldfish swimming in each of them. For myself, I like to listen to a good preacher, and I have no objection in the world to be amused by the tricks of a clever conjurer; but I prefer to keep the conjuring and the preaching separate: conjuring on Sunday morning, conjuring in church, conjuring with texts of Scripture, is not quite to my taste. (*Nine Lectures on Preaching*, the 1876 Yale Lectures [London: Hodder & Stoughton, 1877], p. 127)

3. *The storyteller.* This man has convinced himself that since everyone loves a good story and since people tend to be less inclined to follow the exposition of the Bible, he will develop his gift of storytelling to the neglect of the hard work of biblical exposition. Yes, stories were part of the teaching of Jesus. But the fact that his parables were, as we learned in Sunday school, "earthly stories with heavenly meaning" does not grant the contemporary preacher the license to tell stories devoid of heavenly meaning that are of no earthly use!

4. *The entertainer.* Too often these days one is

invited to preach with no thought given to the preacher being part of the worshiping throng. Instead he is invited to relax "backstage" until it is time for him to "do his thing." I do not want to impugn the motives of those who function in this fashion, but I do question the rightness of such a procedure. It tends to foster an environment in which the people come to sit back, relax, and assess the performance rather than to have the heart-attitude of the hymn writer:

> Master, speak, thy servant heareth,
> Waiting for thy gracious word.
> Speak to me by name, O Master,
> Let me know it is to me.

There is a marked difference in perspective between the joyful solemnity I recall in the vestry at Charlotte Chapel, Edinburgh, in the final moments before it was time to mount the pulpit steps and the "go get 'em" camaraderie in many churches today, the latter being more like a locker room sixty seconds before the kickoff.

5. *The systematizer.* I am referring here to the preacher who views the text of Scripture merely as the backdrop for a doctrinal lecture. This is different from the individual who in the course of exegeting the passage draws out the elements of Christian doctrine. The systematizer's theological framework is so pronounced that it predominates the exposition.

Roy Clements refers to this as the propositional paraphrase sermon, which he says is very likely to lack emotional engagement with the text. "There will be little sensitivity to literary genre. Apocalyptic, poetry, narrative, parable, all are flattened to the prosaic level of a theology text-book. No attempt is made to do justice to the lyrical, dramatic, ironic aspects of the text" ("Expository Preaching in a Postmodern World," *The Cambridge*

Papers, September 1998). Understandably, when we hear this kind of preaching, we do not doubt its truthfulness, but we do wonder at the absence of passion. While we recognize that one's theological framework affects our view of the Bible, we need to work hard to ensure that the Scripture rules our framework, not the other way around.

6. *The psychologist.* This is what we might refer to as airline preaching. In one airline's magazine there is a regular feature provided by a psychologist. I usually read it, and it is almost always to my benefit. I have learned useful tips about bringing up my teenage children and dealing with impatience, and I have been reminded to purchase flowers for my wife. But that's as far as it goes, or should go. Unfortunately, the pulpits of growing numbers of churches are being filled with pseudo-psychologists who have decided to become purveyors of "helpful insights," most of which can be (and often are) delivered without reference to the Bible. It is a kind of "fill in the blank" approach that provides the seven principles for effective fathering or the top ten challenges facing couples today. It is not uncommon to meet individuals who are being malnourished on this kind of diet and to hear them crying rightly, as the people did in Nehemiah's day, "Bring out the Book" (Neh. 8:1).

7. *The naked preacher.* In our "bare all" culture it has become increasingly in vogue for preachers to use the pulpit as a place for sharing their faults and foibles and to make an attempt at "authenticity." By this means they let the people know how "real" they are, as if the people needed help to make such a discovery! If we have been among our people for any length of time, they will have had plenty of occasions to recognize that both we and they are redeemed sinners. The sermon is usually not the best place for such sharing. We have our hands full proclaiming the Gospel, pointing to Christ, telling

the story. It is not advisable to use the time to point to ourselves and share *our* story.

This list is selective and not exhaustive. We will not comment here about "the politician" or "the end-times guru" or "the hobby-horse rider." However, I cannot resist sharing G. Campbell Morgan's story about the Baptist preacher who had a fixation with baptism and referred to it constantly. One morning he announced his text—"Adam, where are you?" (Gen. 3:9). He continued, "There are three lines we shall follow. First, where Adam was. Second, how he was to be saved from where he was. Third and last, a few words about baptism."

TWO

What Happened to Expository Preaching?

Why is expository preaching absent from so many of today's churches? Because of a loss of confidence in the Scriptures, preoccupation with the wrong battles, and a sad lack of excellent role models, many preachers compromise on their calling and revert to the expectations of the culture.

Loss of Confidence in the Scriptures

The absence of expository preaching is directly related to an erosion of confidence in the authority and sufficiency of Scripture. At the beginning of the nineteenth century the battle lines were drawn against the forces of liberalism. Liberals were challenging the miraculous, questioning the divine, and opposing the historicity of the New Testament documents. Evangelicals weathered that storm, and empty liberal churches testify to the futility of the liberal quest for a demythologized Christ. But today the battle is more subtle. The Scriptures are neglected and debased and are used only as a springboard for all kinds of "talks" that are far removed from genuine biblical exposition.

It is very possible to attend a service of worship in an avowedly evangelical congregation and find that if the Bible is read or referred to at all (and there is no guarantee it will be), it is weightless in its influence because of inadequate presentation or emphasis. There is little, if any, sense of either the preacher or the congregation bowing under the majesty authority of God's written Word. We live at a time when being unsure and vague is in vogue. There is a contemporary distrust of anything or anyone who is assured or authoritative. Young pastors particularly may find themselves intimidated in such an environment and begin to preach sermons that have their genesis in what people want to hear rather than in what God has chosen to say and command.

Dick Lucas, pastor of St. Helens Bishopsgate Church, London, highlighted the danger in this approach when he said at one of his pastors' conferences, "The pew cannot control the pulpit. We cannot deliver 'demand led' preaching because no one demands the Gospel."

Exposition of Scripture is also undermined by a fascination with the so-called extra-biblical "prophetic word." I recall a well-known Bible teacher in Britain moving deliberately from the exposition of the Scriptures to the uttering of a "word of prophecy." Having read from the Scriptures, he would close his Bible and preface his remarks with, "This is what God is saying to us now." Even those whose approach is softer risk diverting the listener away from a clear reliance on the sufficiency of Scripture.

Sinclair B. Ferguson wrote of such preaching, "While it is denied that additions are being made to the canon of Scripture, it is nevertheless implied that an actual addition is being made to the canon of living. Otherwise the illumination of Scripture and the wisdom to apply it would be sufficient" (*The Holy Spirit* [Downers Grove, Ill.: InterVarsity Press, 1996], p. 231).

In a similar way, a preoccupation with psychological theory has in many cases eroded confidence in the Scriptures. When the essence of the human predicament is redefined in terms of a lack of self-esteem, it is almost inevitable that people will be directed toward a couch but not a cross, a psychologist but not a Savior. The extent to which this has happened can be gauged by listening to various strange blends of psychology and theology, some of which are even offered as attempts at expository preaching!

Fighting the Wrong Battles

When pastors become convinced that the central issue facing the church is political or psychological rather than theological, exposition will be forsaken in favor of political speeches and calls to wage war for "the soul of the nation." Congregations are then more urged to vote than to pray. They are mobilized not on the basis of a divine mandate, but on the strength of a human agenda.

No twentieth-century preacher has been clearer on this than the late D. Martyn Lloyd-Jones. Preaching in Canada from 1 Thessalonians 1:5, he declared:

> The thing that makes the Christian message a Gospel is that it is a proclamation of the good news. It is not just topical comments on the latest scandal in the newspapers or the latest bit of news. It is not that we spend our time in telling kings and princes and presidents and prime ministers how they ought to be running their countries and how they ought to be solving the international problem. We are not qualified to do so. . . . What was it the Apostle preached about? Did the Apostle preach politics to these people? Did he say to them that it is about time you banded yourselves together and raised an army to rid yourself of the yoke of the Roman Empire? Did he object to taxation? Did he

protest against the various things that were happening? That was not his message at all. (Quoted in Tony Sargent, *The Sacred Anointing* [Wheaton, Ill.: Crossway, 1994], pp. 254, 267)

What was the content of the apostle's preaching? Where did it start? What was its first point? Lloyd-Jones answered, "God!"

Young men beginning pastoral ministry are besieged by members of their congregations wanting them to begin their sermons with man and his need instead of God and his glory. Paranoid preoccupation with a new millennium is due more to a preoccupation with ourselves and our needs than to a humble dependence upon the unerring truth of the Bible. The antidote to such a virulent disease is biblical preaching that allows the Scriptures to establish the agenda.

Lack of Excellent Role Models

I am not saying there are none, but they are few and far between. Most young men leaving seminary and going into pastoral ministry appear to be enamored with dramatic success stories that are driven more by "the market" than by apostolic pattern and precepts. Consequently these are the models that tend to be adopted. Unfortunately, in many of these situations the approach to Bible teaching is hardly expository.

In fairness, we must recognize that such individuals are often taking seriously the need to engage the contemporary culture, a worthy intention. But as we have seen, the weakness in beginning at that point is that we allow the culture rather than the Bible to establish and control our proclamation. Roy Clements wrote, "If we constantly allow the preoccupations of our world to be the launching pad for our preaching, we will certainly miss many vital things God may want to say to us" (*The Cambridge Papers*, September 1998).

On the other side of the fence we discover others, equally mistaken, who claim to know better. They are committed to the faithful exposition of Scripture but are so buried in the text that they are completely divorced from the culture to which they have been called to preach. They are like those John Stott describes who shoot arrows from the island of the biblical text but fail to hit the island of contemporary culture. The arrows go straight up and come down on their own heads. These well-meaning and faithful students of the Word are so tied up in their "systems" that they do not discover what happens when one makes a reasonable attempt to bring together the two horizons of biblical theology and contemporary culture.

One of the reasons for the disinterest in expository preaching is surely that so many attempts at it prove lifeless, dull, and even thoroughly boring. I never cease to be amazed by the ingenuity of those who are capable of taking the powerful, life-changing text of Scripture and communicating it with all the passion of someone reading aloud from the Yellow Pages!

Calvin said of God's work in preaching, "He deigns to consecrate the mouths and tongues of men to his service, making his own voice to be heard in them. Whenever God is pleased to bless their labor, he makes their doctrine efficacious by the power of his Spirit; and the voice, which is in itself mortal, is made an instrument to communicate eternal life" (from *Pulpit and People*, Nigel M. Cameron and Sinclair B. Ferguson, editors [Edinburgh: Rutherford House, 1986]).

Here we see the immeasurable significance of the preacher's task and yet at the same time the antidote to pride. The expositor is God's servant, submitting to and proclaiming the text of Holy Writ.

"The passage itself is the voice, the speech of God; the preacher is the mouth and the lips, and the congregation . . . the ear in which the voice sounds" (Gustaf Wingren, *The Living Word* [London: SCM, 1960], p. 201).

The expositor is not a poet moving his listeners by cadence and imagery, nor is he an author reading from a manuscript. He is a *herald* speaking by the strength and authority of heaven. Fifty years ago James S. Stewart said, and it is still true today: "The disease of modern preaching is its search after popularity."

Expository preaching means unfolding the text of Scripture in a way that makes contact with the listeners' world while exalting Christ and confronting them with the need for action, and we need to identify and emulate role models in this noble pursuit. For me, the men who have led the way (and all of them happen to be from the other side of the Atlantic) are Eric Alexander, Roy Clements, Dick Lucas, Derek Prime, and D. Martyn Lloyd-Jones. Who are yours?

The Results of the Absence of Expository Preaching

To fail to practice expository preaching is not a matter to be taken lightly. There are costly consequences. It may seem that we are speaking too much of the negative in this short volume, but that is only because the matter is so very important.

1. *Confusion.* When Paul wrote to Titus he warned him (and us) about the "many rebellious people, mere talkers and deceivers" who "must be silenced" (Titus 1:10-11). This is clearly the responsibility of the elders. How are they to accomplish this? By a thorough knowledge of the Scriptures and the Gospel. An elder "must hold firmly to the trustworthy message as it has been

taught, so that he can encourage others by sound doctrine and refute those who oppose it" (v. 9).

It is the work of the Word to teach, rebuke, correct, and train so that God's people can set out on the voyage of life equipped for search and rescue. When the Bible is not being systematically expounded, congregations often learn a little about a lot but usually do not understand how everything fits together. They are like workers in a car assembly plant who know how to add their particular component but remain largely clueless as to how it fits in with the rest of the process. The most dangerous people in our churches are those who are susceptible to all kinds of passing fads and fancies; they often prove to be a trial to themselves as well as to others.

It is striking that in a time of great moral and doctrinal confusion, Paul exhorted Timothy not to spend his time learning clever answers to silly questions, but rather to give his time and energy to preaching the Word of God (2 Tim. 4:2-5).

2. *Malnutrition.* As Walter C. Kaiser has written:

> It is no secret that Christ's Church is not in good health in many places of the world. She has been languishing because she has been fed, as the current line has it, "junk food"; all kinds of artificial preservatives and all sorts of unnatural substitutes have been served up to her. As a result, theological and biblical malnutrition has afflicted the very generation that has taken such giant steps to make sure its physical health is not damaged by using foods or products that are harmful to their bodies. Simultaneously a worldwide spiritual famine resulting from the absence of any genuine publication of the Word of God (Amos 8:11) continues to run wild and almost unabated in most quarters of the

Church. (*Toward an Exegetical Theology* [Grand Rapids, Mich.: Baker, 1981], pp. 7-8)

Hebrews 5:12-13 describes those who are stunted in their growth as a result of being stuck on "baby food." John Brown of Haddington comments on their condition: "By their neglect of proper nourishment, they'd spoiled their spiritual appetite, the power of digestion, and had brought themselves to a state of second childhood" (*Hebrews* [Edinburgh and Carlisle, Pa.: Banner of Truth, 1994], p. 269). The Apostle Paul combines both pictures when he mentions "infants, tossed back and forth by the waves, and blown here and there by every wind of teaching and by the cunning and craftiness of men in their deceitful scheming" (Eph. 4:14).

The preventive medicine for this disease is the preaching and teaching ministry that God has established to bring his people to maturity.

THREE

The Nature of Expository Preaching

No treatment of the nature of expository preaching would be complete without referring to the dramatic scene recorded in Nehemiah 8:

> All the people assembled as one man in the square before the Water Gate. They told Ezra the scribe to bring out the Book of the Law of Moses, which the LORD had commanded for Israel. . . . He read it aloud from daybreak till noon as he faced the square before the Water Gate in the presence of the men, women and others who could understand. And all the people listened attentively to the Book of the Law. . . . The Levites . . . instructed the people in the Law while the people were standing there. They read from the Book of the Law of God, making it clear and giving the meaning so that the people could understand what was being read. (vv. 1, 3, 7-8)

The sense of expectation among those people was almost palpable. Can it be wrong for us to long for our people to gather to wait upon the preaching of the Word with the same passion and hunger?

Such a heightened sense of expectation is inevitably tied to a high view of Scripture. There is a dramatic difference between the congregation that gathers in anticipation of a monologue on biblical matters from a kindly fellow and the one that has come expecting that when God's Word is truly preached, God's voice is really heard. Calvin expresses this in his commentary on Ephesians: "It is certain that if we come to church we shall not hear only a mortal man speaking but we shall feel (even by his secret power) that God is speaking to our souls, that he is the teacher. He so touches us that the human voice enters into us and so profits us that we are refreshed and nourished by it. God calls us to him as if he had his mouth open and we saw him there in person" (*Ephesians* [Edinburgh and Carlisle, Pa.: Banner of Truth, 1973], p. 42).

On one occasion a visitor to Gilcomston South Church in Aberdeen, while greeting the minister, William Still, at the conclusion of a service, commented, "But you don't preach." When the pastor asked what he meant, the man answered, "You just take a passage from the Bible and explain what it means." Mr. Still replied, "Brother, that is preaching!"

He and others like him are simply following the pattern for expository preaching established by Ezra and his colleagues. Those godly men read God's Book and explained it, and they did so in such a way that the people understood the implications.

How are we to accomplish this? What are the key principles of expository preaching?

Begin with the Text

Expository preaching always begins with the text of Scripture.

That does not mean every sermon will begin with the phrase, "Please turn in your Bible to . . ." But it does mean that even when we begin by referring to some current event or the lyric of a contemporary song, it is the text of Scripture that establishes the agenda for the sermon. The Bible expositor does not start with an idea or a great illustration and then search for an appropriate passage. Instead he begins with the Scripture itself and allows the verses under consideration to establish and frame the content of the sermon. This is why, as John Stott says, "It is our conviction that all true Christian preaching is expository preaching" (*Between Two Worlds* [Grand Rapids, Mich.: Eerdmans, 1982], p. 125). We are on the wrong track if we think of expository preaching merely as a preaching *style* chosen from a list (topical, devotional, evangelistic, textual, apologetic, prophetic, expository).

Roy Clements says rightly, "Expository preaching is not a matter of style at all. In fact, the determinative step which decides whether a sermon is going to be expository or not takes place, in my view, before a single word has been actually written or spoken. First and foremost, the adjective 'expository' describes the method by which the preacher decides what to say, not how to say it" (*The Cambridge Papers,* September 1998).

Exposition is not simply a running commentary on a passage of Scripture. Nor is it a succession of word studies held loosely together by a few illustrations. We should not even think of it in terms of the discovery and declaration of the central doctrine found in the passage. We can do all that without accomplishing biblical exposition in terms of the definition we are building.

Stand Between Two Worlds

Expository preaching seeks to fuse the two horizons of the biblical text and the contemporary world.

This insight is worked out thoroughly by John Stott in *Between Two Worlds: The Art of Preaching in the Twentieth Century.* Stott argues rightly that it is possible to preach exegetically and yet fail to answer the "so what?" in the listener's mind. Ezra's hearers, for example, would never have begun construction of the booths if he had failed to establish the link between the text and the times. True exposition must have some prophetic dimension that leaves the listener in no doubt that what he has heard is a living word from God and creates in him at least the sneaking suspicion that the Author knows him.

If we are going to take the challenge to teach the Bible in this way seriously, we must pay attention to the warning of a twentieth-century Scottish preacher who said that it is sheer slackness to fling at people great slabs of religious phraseology derived from a bygone age without helping them retranslate the message into their own experience. That is the preacher's task, not theirs, he argued.

The rediscovery of the theological works of the Puritans is something for which we are all grateful; but at the same time the proliferation of young men whose pulpit delivery owes more to the seventeenth century than to the twenty-first should be a cause for concern. Of course, the problem is arguably far more significant at the other end of the spectrum, where we find sermons that are overly steeped in the issues and interests of contemporary culture. Such preaching tends to establish contact with the listener very quickly, but its connection with the Bible is so slight that it fails to establish the link between the world of the Bible and the personal world of the listener. The preacher's task is to declare what God has said, explain the meaning, and establish the implications so that no one will mistake its relevance.

Donald Grey Barnhouse frequently described this task as "the art of explaining the text of the Word of God, using all the experience of life and learning to illuminate the exposition."

Show Relevance

Expository preaching encourages the listener to understand why a first-century letter to the church in Corinth is relevant to a twenty-first-century congregation living in Cleveland.

It is important that the listener does not leave mystified by the way in which the preacher dealt with the text. The preacher must learn not simply to fuse the horizons in his teaching, but to do so in such a way that the people are learning by example how to integrate the Bible with their own experience. Listeners face the twin dangers of assuming either that what they have just heard is totally unrelated to where they are living or that it is *immediately* applicable, that it is "just for them." Allow me to explain further about these two dangers.

1. *That the message is irrelevant.* The preacher must work hard to ensure that he has not simply done good exegesis, helping the listener to understand the meaning of the text, but has also labored to establish its relevance to the listener's personal world. For example, in addressing the doctrine of the incarnation he must not content himself with simply ensuring that his listeners have grasped the instruction but will point out the implications of the great principle of "incarnational mission." To establish that link the preacher may say something along the lines of, "The ministry of Jesus was one of involvement, not detachment; and therefore we must face the fact that we cannot minister to a lost world if we are not in it."

2. *That the message is immediately relevant.* The second danger is just as real. Here the listener wants to move immediately to application. He will be anxious to know "what this means *to me.*" In many cases this rush to personalize the text will be removed from the necessary understanding of what the passage means in its original context.

I know of no one who has been more helpful in getting preachers to wrestle with this than Dick Lucas. Those of us who in presenting our work to a jury of our peers have been brought to an abrupt halt by Dick's, "Come now, dear boy, that's surely not what the apostle means!" will not soon forget the experience. I am very grateful that he has made me wary of trying to apply the text to Cleveland before I have discovered Paul's purpose in addressing the congregation in first-century Corinth.

It is clearly possible, for example, to unearth a text like Hebrews 13:8 ("Jesus Christ is the same yesterday and today and forever") from the surrounding context and do an adequate job of speaking about the benefits to the believer of a Jesus who is unchanging. But if we want our listeners to learn how to interpret the Bible, we must do the hard work of understanding why verse 8 appears between verses 7 and 9. If we do that work, we will find it necessary to explain our verse not simply in isolation or in terms of our immediate context but in the wider context of the book. We will recognize that any application that does not focus on the permanent priesthood of Christ will not only have missed the point but will have done a disservice to our people who are learning with us.

The expositor needs to be under the control of Scripture. This is the third of three principles for faithful exposition provided by the *Westminster Directory for Public Worship*:

1. The matter we preach should be true; that is, in the light of general doctrines of Scripture.

2. It should be the truth contained in the text or passage we are expounding.

3. It should be the truth preached under the control of the rest of Scripture.

What a radical change would come about in pulpits all across the country if we were to take these three principles seriously. We would be forced to ensure that the pulpit did not afford a place for theorizing and speculation, for sloganeering and manipulation, for tall stories and emotionalism. In an earlier era in Scotland when great pains were taken to abide by these principles, the impact was obvious. Indeed, the knowledge of the Bible possessed by our ordinary congregations, amid all our supposed understanding and enlightenment, bears no comparison with that of simple Scottish people of the last generation who were taught from infancy to follow the preacher's teaching from the Bible. Although that was long before my time, the benefit lingered, and I can still recall my father's slightly trembling hand as it held the Bible and his finger guided my gaze along the page. How magnificent it is when God ministers to our hearts through the power of expository preaching!

FOUR

The Benefits of Expository Preaching

There are immense benefits of expository preaching that are not present to the same degree, if at all, in other types of preaching. These alone are compelling arguments as to why genuine expository preaching should be recovered and faithfully practiced in our day. We will now review these benefits.

It Gives Glory to God Alone

Expository preaching gives glory to God, which ought to be the ultimate end of all we do.

The psalmist declares, "You have exalted above all things your name and your word" (Ps. 138:2). Since expository preaching begins with the text of Scripture, it starts with God and is in itself an act of worship, for it is a declaration of the mighty acts of God. It establishes the focus of the people upon God and his glory before any consideration of man and his need. In beginning here we affirm the place of preaching not on the grounds of personal interest but because it pleases God. A congregation that has accepted this and is beginning to learn the implications of it will be markedly different from one in which sermons constantly find their origin in the felt needs of the people.

It Makes the Preacher Study God's Word

Expository preaching demands that the preacher himself become a student of the Word of God.

After seminary, serving in their first church, pastors study to produce a variety of sermons. But some, having preached them all, then move on to give another congregation the benefit of their study. By contrast when a pastor is committed to the systematic and consecutive exposition of Scripture, he will never come to an end of his task. If we are not learning, we are not growing; and if we are stuck, we can be certain that our people will be stuck with us. It is vital that we keep coming to the Scriptures in the spirit of discovery. We must learn to look for the surprises in the passage. We should not assume that we "understand" just because we have spent time in this passage before. Rather, we should always be praying:

> O teach me, Lord, that I may teach
> The precious things Thou dost impart;
> And wing my words that they may reach
> The hidden depths of many a heart.

The first heart God's Word needs to reach is that of the preacher. There will be no benefit to our people from expository preaching unless we ourselves are being impacted by the Scripture we are preparing to preach. It is imperative, when we are dealing with the biblical text, that we are personally changed by it. John Owen spoke of this necessity of experiencing the power of truth in our own souls: "A man only preaches a sermon well to others if he has first preached it to himself. If he does not thrive on the 'food' he prepares, he will not be skilled at making it appetizing for others. If the Word does not dwell in power in us, it will not pass in power from us" (*The Works of John Owen*, vol. 16 [Edinburgh and Carlisle, Pa.: Banner of Truth, 1968], p. 76).

It Helps the Congregation

Expository preaching enables the congregation to learn the Bible in the most obvious and natural way.

We would not expect a university professor to teach from a textbook on the human anatomy by picking out parts of sentences at random and using them for his lecture. Rather, we would anticipate his working through the material in an orderly fashion to ensure that his students come to understand how the pieces fit together.

Many men are capable of delivering excellent orations, producing touching illustrations, and uttering stirring exhortations based on scriptural material but as expositors of Scripture are ineffective. Spurgeon in lectures to his students observed, "I believe the remark is too well grounded that if you attend to a lecturer on astronomy or geology, during a short course you will obtain a tolerably clear view of his system; but if you listen, not only for twelve months, but for twelve years, to the common run of preachers, you will not arrive at anything like an idea of their system of theology" (*Lectures to My Students* [Grand Rapids, Mich.: Zondervan, 1972], p. 71).

By our preaching we either help or hinder our people in the task of interpreting Scripture. If we merely show them the results of our study without at least to some degree including them in the process, they may be "blessed" but will remain untaught. To borrow again from Roy Clements, "It is no longer enough to feed our people. These days we must also show them how to cook."

It Demands Treatment of the Entire Bible

Expository preaching prevents the preacher from avoiding difficult passages or from dwelling on his favorite texts.

This is no small matter. The computer on

which I am presently working has a screen saver. Whenever there has been an absence of activity for any significant length of time, it automatically defaults to one particular image. In a similar fashion, when the preacher has not been active in the systematic study of Scripture, he will find himself defaulting to his pet passages to save face. For some this might be "higher life" teaching or an emphasis on "the risen life of Christ." Others default to flights of eschatological fancy that are guaranteed to intrigue but that seldom manage to instruct. Whatever the emphasis may be, it will in time become an overemphasis, and the congregation will come to expect only that for which the preacher has become known.

By this methodology many congregations are denied the opportunity to wrestle with the mind-stretching, soul-stirring doctrine of election. Others have never examined the issue of spiritual gifts or have managed to avoid consideration of "controversial" subjects like homosexuality, the role of women, or the future of Israel. By committing himself to an exposition of Scripture that is systematic in its pattern, the preacher will avoid these pitfalls.

It Provides a Balanced Diet

Expository preaching assures the congregation of enjoying a balanced diet of God's Word.

This is the reverse of the previous point. Each of us comes to a given text of Scripture with a framework. It may be something as simple as the slogan, "The Old (Testament) is in the New revealed; the New is in the Old concealed." Or it may be, "We find Christ in all the Scriptures. In the Old Testament he is predicted, in the Gospels he is revealed, in the Acts he is preached, in the epistles he is explained, and in the Revelation he is expected." We use such frameworks to help us navigate the Scriptures. Certainly they have value.

However, there is a danger when the framework is more substantial than in the illustrations above. In such a case, instead of the text of Scripture dictating to our framework, whether it is a dispensational or covenant hermeneutic or whatever, we allow the tail to wag the dog.

Also, sometimes the framework is the product of a denominational distinctive that creates an imbalance. For example, I was worshiping in a church in South Carolina where the pastor was doing a series of studies from 1 Timothy. The passage for that morning was the first thirteen verses of the third chapter. In opening up the text he said something like this: "The first seven verses have to do with elders, but since we are Baptists we don't have them. So let's go directly to verse 8, which deals with deacons!"

On another occasion I was worshiping in Grand Rapids, Michigan. The pastor was dealing with the subject of Communion, and I quickly lost track of how many times he urged us to consult the copy of the Heidelberg Catechism sitting before us in the pews. One might have been forgiven for wondering whether the ultimate authority was the Bible or the catechism.

Exposition, which constantly affirms the priority and sufficiency of the text, will prevent such an imbalance from taking place. As a result we risk being regarded as being less than precise on our systematic theology; but we should not be more precise than the text of Scripture allows.

Teaching the Bible in this way should not mean a lack of variety. In fact, the variety inherent in the Bible itself should be present in our preaching. Expository preaching need not be limited to exhaustive and exhausting studies through books of the Bible. Ninety percent of what I do is careful study of particular Bible books, but we can also do character studies or a series on the parables in

Luke or on key Christian doctrines and tackle each of them in an expository form. For example, in preaching on the matter of temptation we can expound the first half of James 1 rather than pulling together material from all over the Bible. We serve our people best when we make clear that we are committed to teaching the Bible *by teaching the Bible!*

It Eliminates Saturday Night Fever

Expository preaching liberates the preacher from the pressure of last-minute preparation on Saturday night.

Expository preaching that is systematic and consecutive in its pattern means that the congregation does not approach church asking themselves, "I wonder what the minister will preach about today?" And the pastor is freed from facing the same question with painful, relentless regularity. From a pragmatic perspective, that alone is enough to convince me of the value of expository preaching.

Following the example of my mentor, Derek Prime, I often take a break in the middle of a long series, perhaps on 1 Corinthians or John's Gospel, by doing a mini-series on something else. This gives the preacher and the people a purposeful pause and allows both to return to the main series with fresh expectation. On a very limited number of occasions I have also interrupted a series in order to address a subject that has gripped the congregation or the nation. But this is different from the all too familiar picture of the pastor in his study on a Saturday evening with his hair disheveled, surrounded by balls of paper, each of which represents a sermon idea that refused to be born. Even the great Spurgeon was often perilously close to this danger. He acknowledged:

To me still, I must confess, my text selection is a very great embarrassment. . . . I confess that I frequently sit hour after hour praying and waiting for a subject, and that this is the main part of my study; much hard labor have I spent in manipulating topics, ruminating upon points of doctrine, making skeletons out of verses and then burying every bone of them in the catacombs of oblivion, sailing on and on over leagues of broken water, till I see the red lights and make sail direct to the desired haven. I believe that almost any Saturday in my life I make enough outlines of sermons, if I felt the liberty to preach them, to last me for a month, but I no more dare to use them than an honest mariner would run to shore a cargo of contraband goods. (*Lectures to My Students,* pp. 84-85)

But Spurgeon was unique, perhaps even a genius. Shall we allow his pattern to overturn the points I have labored to make? I think not. All we need to acknowledge is that God does not come upon methods but upon men, even when our methods may not give the appearance of being the wisest or the best. I have often imagined how grand it would be to be able to turn to volumes of Spurgeon's consecutive exposition rather than the collections of sermons he has actually left to us, as rich as they are. Spurgeon serves as a reminder that the best of men are men at best and that there has only ever been one perfect preacher, and that is Jesus.

FIVE

Practical Pointers

I have always been fascinated by the variety of approaches that preachers take in preparing their sermons. In our delivery, and in our preparation, we must "to our own selves be true." Some have a unique facility of memory; others are expert in the use of technology. Some of us are still working with legal pads and pencils. Probably the only factor that we all share is that we come to the text upon our knees, at least figuratively. The attitude of heart with which we come to our preparation should express our dependence upon God.

Whenever I am asked to summarize my own method of preparation, I mention the following points, which I learned from an older minister when I was still a theological student.

Think Yourself Empty

It is helpful if we can survey the passage in a proper spirit of unlearnedness. We do not want to be uncertain by the time our study ends, but it is all right and often beneficial to avoid the proud assumption that we know initially what everything means. Obviously as time passes, we will have a greater grasp of more and more material, but it is always good to train our minds to expect the unexpected. This will open up new avenues of thought and create angles of approach that we may never have seen before. In this stage I write down anything that comes to mind—parallel passages, possible illustrations, textual difficulties, poems, hymn quotes, a sketchy outline if it emerges naturally. Much of what goes on that initial page will never become part of the sermon, but that doesn't matter. The humbling part of this is when it takes only five minutes to think ourselves empty and there is very little to show for it on the largely empty page!

The point is, if we do not become thinking pastors, we are unlikely to have thinking congregations.

Read Yourself Full

The pastor should read widely and regularly. There are certain books we should return to routinely: Baxter's *The Reformed Pastor*, Augustine's *Confessions*, and, as daunting as we may find it, Calvin's *Institutes*. I also find great profit in reading biographies. The two volumes on Lloyd-Jones should be a prerequisite for all pastors, as well as at least the first volume on Whitefield by Arnold Dallimore. There is also profit in the biographies of politicians, musicians, golfers, and various others. (I betray here my personal interests.) Novels that pass the Philippians 4:8 test are also helpful. Along with this I personally am helped by book reviews in the *New York Times*, and even the obituaries. As time allows, it is also important to read material from competing perspectives. This helps us sharpen our wits and keeps us on our theological toes.

In reading about the text from which we are about to preach, there are many useful resources: *The New International Commentary* on both the Old and New Testaments, Lenski on the New Testament, the Hendriksen commentary series, and many more. We must learn to benefit from these resources without becoming tied to them or allowing their insights to rob us of the necessary personal experience of discovery and creativity.

Write Yourself Clear

Aside from the essential empowering of the Holy Spirit, if there is one single aspect of sermon preparation that is most closely tied to fluency of speech and impact in delivery, it is this: Freedom of delivery in the pulpit depends upon careful organization in the study. We may believe that we have a grasp of the text and that we are clear about our delivery, only to stand up and discover that somewhere between our thinking and our speaking things have gone badly awry. The missing link can usually be traced to the absence of putting our thoughts down clearly.

James S. Stewart tells the story of a young minister who, concerned about the apparent failure of his preaching, consulted Dr. Joseph Parker in the vestry of the City Temple. His sermons, he complained, were producing only apathy. Could Dr. Parker frankly tell him what was lacking? "Suppose you preach me one of your sermons now," said Parker. His visitor, not without some trepidation, complied. When it was over, Parker told him to sit down. "Young man," he said, "you asked me to be frank. I think I can tell you what is the matter. For the last half hour you have been trying to get something out of your head instead of something into mine!"

When we take the time to commit not only our thoughts but our sentences and paragraphs and linking phrases to paper, we will quickly detect the *non sequiturs* and be able to make corrections long before we are presenting the material in a public forum. When a speaker gives the impression that he is working out what he is trying to say as he is speaking, he probably is!

In most cases both the speaker and the listeners will be helped by some kind of outline, and this generally emerges in the writing stage, if not before. But the preacher and the congregation should both only be helped to think clearly, not overpowered by the cleverness or weight of the outline. Eric Alexander observes, "The structure must never obtrude so as to be admired for its cleverness or originality. It needs to represent the content of the passage and must never be an ill-fitting box into which the truth is thrust, as if we are more concerned with the packaging than with the content. It is the finished building men want to see and not the builder's scaffolding" ("Plainly Teaching the Word," unpublished message delivered to the Toronto Spiritual Life Conference, January 10, 1989).

Pray Yourself Hot

There is no chance of fire in the pews if there is an iceberg in the pulpit; and without personal prayer and communion with God during the preparation stages, the pulpit will be cold. When the apostles did some reorganization of the early church, it was because they realized how crucial it was for them to give themselves continually to "prayer and the ministry of the word" (Acts 6:4). To borrow from the marriage ceremony, it is imperative that "what God has joined together, no man should put asunder." We dare not divorce our preaching from our praying.

In an ordination sermon preached in Bridgewater, Massachusetts, in 1752, John Shaw reminded the incumbent pastor:

> If any men in the world need the special presence of God with them, and his blessing in order to succeed, certainly ministers do. For what is the design and end of their ministry? Is it not to open the eyes of sin-

ners, to turn them from darkness to light, and from the power of sin and Satan to God in Christ? And "who is sufficient for these things?" In a work of this nature, what can ministers, of themselves, do? Verily, they may preach even to paleness and faintness, until the bellows are burnt, until their lungs and vitals are consumed, and their hearers will never be the better; not one sinner will be converted until God is graciously pleased, by the efficacious working of his Spirit, to add his blessing to their labors and make his Word, in the mouth of the preacher, sharper than any two-edged sword in the heart of the hearer. All will be in vain, to no saving purpose, until God is pleased to give the increase. And in order to do this, God looks for their prayers to come up to his ears. A praying minister is in the way to have a successful ministry. (*The Character of a Pastor According to God's Heart Considered* [Morgan, Pa.: Soli Deo Gloria, 1992], p. 10)

We can do more than pray, after we have prayed, but not until. How easy it is to affirm this, and yet how difficult to practice.

Be Yourself, but Don't Preach Yourself

There is nothing quite so ridiculous as the affected tone and adopted posture of the preacher who wishes he was someone else. Sadly, it is common to listen to someone preach, recognize the tone of voice and the style of delivery, and know that it does not conform to the individual who is preaching. While we can and must learn from those whom God has used to great effect in the pulpit, our admiration dare not lead to imitation.

James Stewart used to say, "Be yourself, but also, forget yourself!" Self-forgetfulness is of vital importance. We cannot make much of ourselves and much of the Lord Jesus Christ simultaneously. If people leave worship saying, "What an amazing preacher!" we have failed. Instead we must long for them to say, "What a great God, and what a privilege it is to meet him in his Word, as we have just done." A good teacher clears the way, declares the way, and then gets out of the way.

We dare not miss the seriousness of this. Three hundred years ago Richard Baxter chided pastors he knew for behaving so "weakly, unhandsomely, imprudently and so slightly" when they were entrusted by God with delivering a message of eternal consequences to the souls of men. We must be warned of this too, and never more so than when we are guilty of pretense. If God has made us a piccolo, we should be content to play our part; if a tuba, then let us strike those low notes with authority. But let not the cello seek to imitate or envy the French horn. We must play the notes prepared for us . . . and always in the key of *B natural!*

May God bless each of us as we seek to serve him and our congregations through expository preaching—preaching done in his way for his glory!

SIX

"Who Is Equal to Such a Task?"

In this high and sacred calling—the task of expository preaching—we are to be men of spiritual wisdom and understanding in the mysteries of the Gospel. We must each have a genuine experience of the power of the truth we proclaim. It is incumbent upon us to be able to divide the Word correctly and to feed the sheep as we discern their condition by spending time among them. There must be about us a zeal for the glory of God and a compassion for the souls of men. And yet, do we not find ourselves exclaiming, "Who is equal to such a task?" (2 Cor. 2:16).

The awesome sense of wonder and privilege described above must have captured the mind of James Henley Thornwell, who wrote: "Depend upon it that there is but little preaching in the world, and it is a mystery of grace and of divine power that God's cause is not ruined in the world when we consider the qualifications of many of its professed ministers to preach it. My own performances in this way fill me with disgust. I have never made, much less preached, a sermon in my life, and I am beginning to despair of ever being able to do it" (quoted by D. Martyn Lloyd-Jones, *Preaching and Preachers,* p. 99). These are not the words of an inept and diffident herald. Thornwell was greatly used.

After preaching for thirty years and judged by many to be the greatest preacher of Reformed theology in the twentieth century, Lloyd-Jones sounded remarkably like Thornwell when he reflected: "Any man who has had some glimpse of what it is to preach will inevitably feel that he has never preached. But he will go on trying, hoping that by the grace of God one day he may truly preach" (*Preaching and Preachers,* p. 99).

As we go on trying, there is no prayer that ought to be more constantly on our lips than that of Charles Wesley:

> *O thou who camest from above*
> *The pure celestial fire to impart,*
> *Kindle a flame of sacred love*
> *On the mean altar of my heart.*
> *There let it for thy glory burn*
> *With inextinguishable blaze.*

Lord, hear our prayer, and let our cry come unto thee. Amen.

FOR FURTHER
READING

Baxter, Richard. *The Reformed Pastor.* Edinburgh and Carlisle, Pa.: Banner of Truth, reprint 1974.

Lloyd-Jones, D. Martyn. *Preaching and Preachers.* Grand Rapids, Mich.: Zondervan, 1971.

Logan, Samuel T., editor. *The Preacher and Preaching: Reviving the Art in the Twentieth Century.* Phillipsburg, N.J.: Presbyterian and Reformed, 1986.

Piper, John. *The Supremacy of God in Preaching.* Grand Rapids, Mich.: Baker, 1990.

Spurgeon, Charles Haddon. *An All-Round Ministry.* Edinburgh and Carlisle, Pa.: Banner of Truth, reprint 1960.

Spurgeon, Charles Haddon. *Lectures to My Students,* new edition containing selected lectures from series 1, 2, and 3. Grand Rapids, Mich.: Zondervan, 1972.

Stott, John R. W. *Between Two Worlds: The Art of Preaching in the Twentieth Century.* Grand Rapids, Mich.: Eerdmans, 1982.